FLUID STATES

Heidi Czerwiec

FLUID STATES

Robert C. Jones Short Prose Series
Warrensburg, Missouri

Library of Congress Control Number:
ISBN 978-0-8071-7059-5

Published by Pleiades Press

Department of English
University of Central Missouri
Warrensburg, Missouri 64093

Distributed by Louisiana State University Press

Cover Image: Lorraine Shemesh, "Lung" 2013. 67 1/2 x 53 1/2
inches, oil on canvas, courtesy Gerald Peters Gallery, New York City.
Book design by Sarah Nguyen
Author's photo by Britta Trygstad

First Pleiades Printing, 2019

Financial support for this project has been provided by the University
of Central Missouri and the Missouri Arts Council, a state agency.

Table of Contents

DECANTS

FUME

Flash prose, in China, is termed a "smoke-long story" for the time, the term, it takes – through smoking a cigarette – to read. The time it takes to breathe in these brief pieces on perfume, *per fume*, through smoke.

USE IT AND/OR LOSE IT

Tonight, to write this, I place a few precious drops of *Chypre de Coty* on my wrist – two fewer drops in my quarter-milliliter vial – two fewer drops in the world of perfume. In the world, period. Two decadent drops that fill the room with its scent warmed by my arm as it evaporates, lost forever. A melancholy smell that, while with you, is nonetheless thinking of somewhere, somewhen else.

One allure of perfume, for me, is the attempt to capture the scent of bygone eras. Vintage perfumes, discontinued or reformulated beyond recognition, exist in fragile spaces – a deceased aunt's abandoned vanity, a forgotten drawer, a box at a garage sale. They don't make 'em like they used to – either the bottles or the perfumes – and glass collectors often obtain the exquisite crystal or cut-glass flasks only to toss the juice inside.

If you use it, you lose it. But if you don't use it, you lose it, too. A catch-22 of limited supplies versus oxidation. Your best solution is to use the perfume as intended: for your own pleasure. And so, the precious drops, applied.

How often vintage scents have dropped their top notes, go straight for the heart. *Chypre de Coty*, the Ur-chypre, has lost its sparkling citrus

11

and bergamot opener. Yet the lavish base of oakmoss – possible only pre-IFRA's restrictions – retains its inky bitterness, a tear-stained love letter, its sadness sustained by vetiver and a disquiet of civet. *Chypre*, anagram for *cypher*, the mysterious source for so many classic scents including, famously, the basis for my beloved *Mitsouko* – in straits, Coty sold the formula to Guerlain in 1919, to which the latter added the voluptuousness of peach.

How disconsolate am I that I will never smell that *Mitsouko*, Diaghilev's choice to douse the velvet drapes of Les Ballets Russes before performances, though I adore the viscous midcentury versions I've acquired online. I will never smell Roja Dove's homage to this story, a scent named *Diaghilev*. I likely will never smell *Djedi* or *Parure, Detchema, Shalini, Inoui—*

But tonight, after I write this, I will lie in bed, try not to sleep, not to miss a moment of this fragrance's unfolding,

> wrist pressed to nose, breathe
> all trace of scent, to preserve
> inside me till spent.

CUIR

Scent and leather go hand in glove. *Leather* is an old word, much unchanged, for the hides of dead beasts. The Guild of Gantiers rode the gauntlet of leather goods, and required nauseous quantities of nitrogenous piss to preserve, sterilize, and tan their hides pliable. Medieval streets ran with nitrogenous piss, and a gloved hand attempting to smother the smell only brought it closer to the nose. Thus death gives birth to French perfumery, decay and disgust disguised by violets and lavender, iris and musk.

An irony: originally used to cover up leather, perfume ultimately comes to emulate it: a barber's razor strap, the smell of a saddle, a tobacco-and-bourbon-imbued library full of leatherbound books. Cured becomes *cuir*, the luxurious floral leathers of Russia and Tuscany and Morocco, expensive purses and vintage touring cars vaguely jasmine-scented as if spritzed by a light hand. And from *cuir* to *queer*, the veneer of sweat-stained chaps and battered motorcycle jackets, leather's skin-on-skin action, the smack of its animalic source.

The kink and kin of skin permeated by skin: where does the leather end and mine begin? *Boxeuses'* broken-in boxing glove fisting your nose. *Diorling* a cruel mistress all but dear, while *Scandal* and *Bandit* crack their quinolines across tender skin. A nearly-noxious romp through Ringling with *Dzing!* And *Cuir de Russie*, a countess stealing a discreet smoke, then applying a fresh coat of lipstick plucked from her leather clutch.

Another irony: while perfume can scent leather, leather cannot scent perfume. There exists no extract of it. What we smell as leather is actually the smell of elements used to tan and scent leather, created by playing chords of perfume notes, to create what is called an accord. The left hand plays a baseline of birchtar, patchouli, vetiver, styrax, and iris. The right hand in turn may finger more feral notes of beaver gland and labdanum. Or, refined with vanilla or fruit, may

> tune leather softer,
> a leather note more mute, sueded,
> played with kid gloves.

EAU'D TO *DIORLING*

The scent clutches you to it.

The scent makes you clutch your pearls, a strand of baroques big as a clutch of eggs.

The smell of a lady's leather clutch, laden with lipstick and compact.

Check your mirror. Click it closed, click your heels.

Check your mirror, its reflection of you in a leather interior. Ease your suede heel off the clutch as you peel out.

COGNOSCENTI: GERMAINE CELLIER

Verde que te quiero verde.
—Federico García Lorca

Germaine Cellier, foremost female "nose," a woman working in perfumery when all perfumers were Master, not mistress, despite women's more sensitive sense of scent. Germaine – meaning "German," a Frankish people – was born in Bordeaux to a would-be Bohemian artist and a melancholy herbalist.

Alchemical, she discovered a natural ability with formulas and structures, how chemistry + narrative = perfume, how a story grabs you with its top notes but engages you with its heart, all the while the base notes provide a satisfying backdrop of setting and scene. She debuted producing basenotes for DuPont in the *cellier*, the storeroom. Then came the Great War.

Then afterwards, a regrowth, as of new green germinating. The Forties a fertile era for her, though she budded best on her own - unwilling to work with the male perfumers, she was granted her own lab where, unlike those who composed perfumes according to charts, she flung fragrance like a Fauve, adding ingredients by the ladleful, painting notes in Expressionist colors, where juxtaposed components fight and fuck within your nose. An aggression of aroma. A dissonance of scent.

Germaine means "armed." In '44, her *Bandit* strong-armed its way on the scene with its nose-searing 1% quinoline, the leathery bitterness a kiss she blew "to the dykes." Then

> *Vent Vert*'s gale-force, the
> galbanum galvanizing,
> its stun-gun of green.

'48's *Fracas* "for the femmes," a buzz up the nose of buttery tuberose – but Germaine means "loud" and it's not a room-clearer for naught. And *Jolie Madame*, a leather so green it hurts the head to contemplate even as you swoon. Green her germ, her cell, her scented vernacular.

She was famous, while composing her fragrances, for chainsmoking Gauloises and consuming quantities of garlic, breakfasting on sardines. Germaine, loud and outspoken, swore fluently and wore fluid Cossack pants, though ne'er a brassiere.

Eventually so much incendiary scent, chemicals, and inhaled smoke germinated in the cells of her lungs, inflamed them, burning off what remained of greenness. What's green smokes most. What's germane are the perfumes that remain, encellared, precious. The smell, indelible, pervades everything.

PROHIBITION EXPEDITION: STEPPING OUT

In the infancy of the Twentieth Century, perfumers colluded to conceal the peccadillos of Jazz Babies. Smoking in the speakeasies, poised with cigarette holders to avoid the telltale nicotine stains, they flaunted drop-waisted dresses to defeminize the figure, drinking like a man as they danced the Lindy Hop. Their fragrance gave cover, camouflaging them in scents heavy with leather, tobacco, and boozy blue notes of bourbon and junipery gin – the Caron of *Tabac Blond* and the Charon of Hades interchangeable; let Lanvin's *My Sin* be your guide.

Drenched in scent, could your mother tell
if you smelt of perdition, or only Chanel?

5 BY (N°) 5

"...to-day there is no man capable of launching a Chanel No. 5."
—Edmond Roudnitska, "Where Are We Going?" (Nov. 1967)

N° 1: Origin Story, or, The Scented Déjeuner [1920]

The invitation to the fashionable café on the Riviera near Grasse contained the curious request to attend in stylish attire, but otherwise unperfumed. When her guests arrived, she seated them at a charming table *au plein air* – elegantly decorated, but bare of flowers – nearest the promenade. They were surprised and delighted when their diminutive hostess spritzed each of them with a new perfume she was testing, oddly named only by number. Soon, sun- and wine-warmed, the scent hovered among them, expanded to envelop passers-by – enchanted, they stopped in their tracks, turned back to track its source. *What is that fragrance? Where can I find it?*

An aperitif of sparkling aldehydes, followed by rose and jasmine served on a bed of sandalwood, and concluded with a light dollop of creamy vanilla.

They hadn't known such
hunger for this smell until,
        devoured, it filled them.

19

It launched on the fifth day of the fifth month. To thank her garden party, she gifted them a precious bottle each. Her best friend Misia confessed, *It was like a winning lottery ticket.*

N° 2: *Sacre Cinq* [5/5/1922]

Cinq similar to *sacre:* the cinqfoil roses above Aubazine convent where she spent her unmothered girlhood.

The five wounds made in an incarnate god; the five sorrows of his fleshed mother.

The body's five senses.

The pentacle made by DaVinci's Vitruvian Man; the number of Man.

Mademoiselle Chanel was fascinated by Madame Blavatsky's theosophy, its individualized mysticism; five became her lucky number.

N° 3: Iconic [1960]

Interviewer: What do you wear to bed?
Marilyn Monroe: Only five drops of Chanel N° 5.

Because of Marilyn, the Hollywood icon, we thought of Chanel N° 5, the perfume icon, thought its boxy bottle a contrast to her curves and bottle blonde. Composed in the Roaring Twenties, the scent allowed Coco to strike a balance between purity and decadence, its formula a sort of autobiography of her convent school's crisp, soapy aldehydes and the innocence of vanilla wherein dwelled the virginal Gabrielle, the luxurious rose soliflores of the ladies she admired and aspired to, and the indolic jasmine and civet of the demimondes and mistresses of which she was one, all enflasked in a whiskey decanter like that favored by a lover she dubbed "Boy." An instant success with the New Woman, it survived by exclusivity, desire its sole advertisement, until the fragrance tainted by Coco's unsavory association with the fishy Vichy government. To stave off bad exposure for treasonous activities, she gave away free bottles to American GIs, the scent the ultimate French souvenir for soldiers' sweethearts Stateside.

Because of Marilyn suggesting the image of herself naked as the day she was born, the star's sultriness scrubbed Chanel's image clean as a baby. Marilyn's boudoir-wear of just five drops of N° 5 – naked throat (left, right), naked cleavage, naked wrists (left, right) – left imaginations reeling at the thought of clean-scrubbed Norma Jean transformed into a new woman and scented for her famous lovers. Thus, the two icons forever fused.

Because of Marilyn, and like Marilyn, Chanel N° 5 is a cultural artifact so instantly identifiable both she and it appear in Andy Warhol's pop-art prints: Marilyn's smile like silk; Chanel's screen of scent.

And yet, because of Marilyn, their best advertising campaign has failed Chanel – everyone's grandmother and mother wore it, a tainted association that deflates its sex appeal. Despite deliberately restricted advertising that nonetheless fanned demand, by 1990 more money was spent to promote it than any other brand. No ad campaign could save it: not Catherine Deneuve, not Nicole Kidman nor Brad Pitt, could recapture that Hollywood glamor of Marilyn. Not even Marilyn, again the image of Chanel thanks to digital manipulation in the new millennium. An icon too iconic – a five-pointed star

      collapsing into
itself – a sex supernova
      self-consuming.

N° 4: False Idols [2016]

Especially in vintage form, $N° 5$ is the most faked fragrance on eBay. Counterfeit labels printed unembossed and affixed askew, looking askance, begging the question. Missing manufacturing information, unpapered and therefore unpedigreed. Bottles unsealed and siphoned off, filled with the weaker eau de cologne or just eau de colored eau. *Oh well – no guarantees with vintage juice,* they shrug. The bold don't bother to hide it, brag on Google: bottled in Hong Kong, sent from Russia, with love.

N° 5: [1990, 1991]

A boy I loved and favored for a lover took me to prom twice. The first time, I wore black satin overlaid with black lace. The second time, I wore red satin, gathered and draped as though wrapped in a post-coital bedsheet. Both times, I wore Chanel N° 5, borrowed from my mother's boudoir since my own everyday scent – *Anaïs Anaïs* – despite evoking a favorite eroticist, smelt too candy-sweet. The Chanel felt stately, grown-up, untouchable.

> I wanted the boy
> to touch me, wrap me in his sheets;
> he never did.

COGNOSCENTI: EDMOND ROUDNITSKA

"Anyone can make a nice smell. The trick is to create a fragrance that has soul."

Rudnik is Russian for "mine," and Roudnitska, Ukrainian émigré, mined the world's fragrant sources to extract their sole scents, their scented souls, scent-signs that combine to create a Transcented Signified, an Ars Parfumica.

Roudnitska thrived on the rude, mining beauty out of barrenness, loveliness from muck, from luck, from lack: "I created Rochas *Femme* in 1943 during the worst days of the war in a building that had a rubbish dump on one side and a paint factory on the other." Tinted a toxic orange, it nonetheless smells lush, seductive but cruel – dry wood and the skins of plums, a woman's skin, a ravishing beauty raised from a razed city out of what remains remained at hand.

Thanks to the income from the phoenix of *Femme* he established his private laboratory Art et Parfum in 1946, moved it to a rocky, barren ground, lost on the heights of Grasse near Cabris, transformed in the course of years into a lush garden full of rare trees and flowering plants. There, he composed perfumes for Dior, including *Diorissimo* (1956), based on lily of the valley, which cannot be extracted; Roudnitska circumvented the scent with synthetics, a master of form.

One Platonic form he kept secret in his cave, his Plutonic treasure, his mine boarded over to warn off all trespassers: *Le Parfum de Thérèse*, a play between dark animalic notes and bright pepper, melon, and jasmine extracts – shadows that never quite come into the light. During his lifetime, only one woman could wear it: his wife, the eponymous Thérèse.

So like a man,
to mark his *femme* with scent, as if
to say she is *mine*.

FLUID

Scents didn't used to be gendered, were fluid as parfum, until (m)ad men's marketing added "pour homme" to perfume. Like most lovers, I swing both ways; as a woman this is easy, the way women have raided men's closets since the closeted 20th Century. Yes, leather and vetiver are easier for a woman to wear, than for a man to gild himself with lily of the valley.

And yet, scents don't
    have genders, any more than
        a garden, an ocean.

PLEASURE / PAIN / *PAMPLELUNE*

My friend recoils –
  to her nose, the bitter grapefruit note
    reads as cat piss.

FLOATING WORLD

At times, in a crowd, I'll catch a scent. As in cartoons, where characters
follow a scent trail as though it's physical –

> I float along on fragrance,
>   phantom hand tickling,
>   beckoning the nose.

Carried through the air, I land at its source: startled and delighted by
the trail she's created.

"GREEN THOUGHT IN A GREEN SHADE"

When younger, I experienced mild synaesthesia where some smells smelled green – only that color, but intense and heady when it happened. I think that's why I'm drawn to green scents: *Vent Vert*, Chanel N° 19, *Silences*. I loved the sense so much I married young a young man whose personal smell was a vivid viridescence.

At 30, my
 synaesthesia failed. At 30
  this first marriage failed.

FRAGRANT FAUX PAS

Have you ever had the sensation of having selected the wrong scent?

Not scrubbers – those smells that screech against your skin, leave you reaching for the soap, the toner, the sandpaper.

Rather, perfumes you love – old friends, signature scents, wardrobe staples, favorite frags.

Sometimes I'll have selected and sprayed myself with a scent, even one I love,

>   not only my throat
> and wrists – hair, cleavage, all my
>   sweet etceteras –

then regretted it. Not the mood I was in, nor the persona I intended to project, or the sillage fills up too much sensory space when I'm feeling more reticent. I deal with dissonance all day.

Last night I wore Chanel N° 19, gorgeous, but too aggressive and steely – its iciness an iteration of the sleet in the streets, its cold metallic hiss isolating when I craved connection. I should have submitted to my first impulse: either *Vol de Nuit* or *Cuir Beluga,* their luxurious embrace of vanilla and leather, their warmth.

Or in heat, in the heat of summer's hormonal flux, the indolic floral I chose rose in my throat, gagging me with the same jasmine I usually use to lull myself to sleep.

So I deal with the dissonance all day,

> the scent a regret
> > that clings like a cloak,
> > > a second skin I can't shed.

THE LOVE FOR THREE ORANGES

In 1918, Prokofiev wrote *The Love for Three Oranges*, a surrealist opera-ballet featuring figures from Commedia del'arte – a comic absurdity, an earnest satire – fairy princesses popping out of giant oranges as if cocooned. A 1988 production added to the music, dance, and visual spectacle, distributing scratch-and-sniff cards scented to accompany the story at various points: a whiff of sulfur for a gunshot, a fart by the Fool Truffaldino, and the scent of oranges.

Now, the fourth wall, bro-
ken completely by language,
its utter attempts.

Aether's Love for Three Oranges [2015]

Inspired by the scratch-and-sniff cards at Prokofiev's opera, Amber Jobin created a scent to encompass all three aspects of orange: fruit, blossom, and tree. Wearing it, I become

bird, concealed among
glossy leaves in an orange tree
abloom and fruiting.

Serge Lutens' Fleurs d'Oranger [1995]

Sweetness of blossoms
paired with salty, sunwarmed skin:
hot flesh after sex.

L'Artisan Parfumeur's Seville à L'Aube [2012]

A perfume blogger and perfumer collaborated to create this erotic scent-memory: embracing a Spanish lover under orange trees brimming with bees during a Holy Week procession.

I'm a perfume collector, and my son Wyatt is irresistibly attracted to my many bottles and samples, loves sniffing their contents alongside me. While not a connoisseur of the orientals and leather scents I prefer, he's partial to florals, orange blossom and jasmine in particular. He often pleads for a spritz. I often grant it. We choose a bottle – his tastes are young, and he's swayed by a flashy flaçon or brightly-colored juice – say, *Seville à L'Aube,* an orange fluid in a dramatic octagonally-cut glass bottle. I uncap it, spray him lightly. I spray myself too, and we enjoy the greeny orange blossom scent warmed with honey as I rub my arms against his, perfuming him, marking him with my scent like an animal, making him mine.

I say, *Tell the bees*
my heart overflows with
sorrowful wax.

DJEDI [1926]

Someone scores a priceless bottle, vintage 1927, offers a sample: just a drop or two at the bottom of a tiny tube, sold for a princely sum. Which you spend.

It arrives. For days, you only gaze at it, attempt to sniff it through the glass, up near the stopper, to avoid opening it, using it up. You read what little description is available to prepare yourself, so when the time comes, you can attempt to appreciate it on as many levels as possible before it vanishes, gone forever.

Created by Jacques Guerlain, inspired by the discovery of Tutankhamun's tomb, and named for an Egyptian magician famed for resurrecting the dead, *Djedi* is stark departure, alien, anti-Guerlain, sucked dry of all voluptuary, what Roja Dove described as "the driest perfume of all time."

And so, you select a humid night to extend the scent, and apply it.

Mineral. Medicinal. Smoke curling from a stone bowl at the limbic, liminal doorway to a tomb. Outside, the smell of dry, reedy vetiver carried on a hot wind blowing over sunbaked bones. And something animalic – a jackal, sinuous in the background. An ephemeral ghost raised briefly from the past.

And though you stay awake as long as possible, you descend to dreams, disquieted. In the morning, *Djedi* has dissipated like smoke:

> distant country
you can never again visit,
> > sunk beneath the sand.

EKPHRAGRANCE

Master perfumer Edmond Roudnitska believed some perfumes achieve a new and beautiful form more than mere sum of its materials. New York's Museum of Art and Design seems to agree, recently hosting an exhibit "The Art of Scent 1889-2011," featuring twelve key scents portraying a range of styles: from *Jicky* and *N° 5*, to *L'Interdit*, to *Pleasures* and *Angel*.

If an art, not an objet d'art, but a temporo-spatial performance. Site-specific, too: taking place in the space surrounding a woman's skin.

And if art, is this essay ekphrasis?

Description

A list of notes – jasmine, bergamot, musk – with an evolution of how they unfold to the nose. Sometimes rendered as impressions, as Impressionism – like Guerlain's soft-focus reveries *Apres L'Ondée* ("after the rainshower") and *L'Heure Bleue* ("the blue hour") – the Surrealism of Thierry Mugler's *Angel*, or Serge Lutens' *postmodernist* (which is to say clever but unlovely) *Laine de Verre* ("fiberglass"). An olfactory art about a visual art.

Narrative

I'm a sucker for the stories associated with scents. It doesn't change the fragrance, but it may capture the persona I wish to project. To be honest, it totally changes the fragrance, makes me love it more.

In the dawn of Modernism, a plane takes off from Paris for Buenos Aires. Suddenly, a storm, all radio contact lost. Every second takes the recently married pilot a little farther from his beloved. *Vol de Nuit* is a perfume of mystery, an homage to writer and aviator Antoine de Saint-Exupéry, who himself disappeared mysteriously.

The story of Parfums Caron is a story of secret love. Daltroff hired former dressmaker Felicie Wanpouille as artistic adviser, but instead she became his muse: supposedly smitten with her, he never formally declared his love. This unrequited undercurrent resulted in some of the 20th century's most tumultuous perfumes: the darkly demented *Narcisse Noir*, the melancholic *N'Aimez Que Moi* ("love no one but me").

Shalimar celebrates the love story of Mughal Emperor Shah Jahan and his third wife, Mumtaz Mahal. The fragrance is named from the famous Shalimar Gardens an earlier Mughal emperor created for a favored concubine homesick for the flora of Kashmir. They also inspired the gardens surrounding Mumtaz' tomb, the Taj Mahal, a memorial to love.

Madeleine-Moments

When I was nineteen, the most exotic person I ever met wore this scent. Everything in her little studio – from her satin sheets to her Persian rugs to her '40s vintage housedresses – smelled of it. She was French, wore fire-red nails and long scarves, brewed us espresso in a crusty old Bialetti. When I first sniffed a sample of vintage Rochas *Femme*, it all came back to me –

scent's molecules sent
straight to the limbic brain,
memory's short circuit.

Vanilla, marzipan: *I smell sex and candy.* The latest fruity-patchouli yawn: *I have no imagination and wish to smell like the celebrity du jour.* Vetiver, oakmoss, muguet, tea: *I'm cautious, contemplative, introverted.* Tuberose, lily: *you will notice me.* Tobacco, cedar, fig: *I want to snuggle.* Galbanum, leather accords: *I'm feeling confident, aggressive.* Civet, labdanum, styrax, musk: *let's fuck.*

BEAR

The handmade sign at the Lupine Meadows trailhead at Grand Teton National Park says an immature grizzly has been sighted in the vicinity, between Jenny and Surprise Lakes – the former named for the beloved wife of a nineteenth-century beaver trapper. Hikers are reminded to keep at least a football-field's length away, since bears can run two to three times faster than humans, and can climb trees. "Be Bear Aware!" is scrawled cheerfully across the bottom.

You are with A__, your first husband, who carries camera equipment – a manual-focus film camera; a bag with extra film, filters (UV, star), and lenses (wide-angle, zoom); and a full tripod – but less than the recommended gallon of water minimum per person. He never asked you to carry extra water for him, but knows you will, because you worry. He bought the camera for himself for his thirtieth birthday. Moving out west has brought out his inner *National Geographic* geek, and he wants to be an explorer, a photographer, wants to use the anthropology degree he is not using at his job at a medical lab. Now that he's seen the sign, he wants a picture of this grizzly. He never asked if you're picturing your skull inside the grizzly's jaw, but knows you will, because you worry. To ease your worry, to make you laugh, he says "*Grand Teton* means *big titty*" and grins.

§

Be aware means beware.

§

Grizzly bears *(Ursus arctos horribilus)* are a species of North American brown bear known for the great hump of their shoulders and for their large size. An adult male can grow to 850 pounds, his shoulders more than a yard high; his paws are nearly a foot in length, larger than a human head, comprised of five digits with six-inch claws. Their jaws, while not long, have a bite pressure of 1,200 pounds per square inch, can chomp through young pine trees. They've been clocked at speeds of up to 35 miles per hour.

§

The trail up Grand Teton, leading to Surprise and Amphitheater Lakes with a view of the frying-pan-shaped Middle Teton Glacier, is steep and switchbacked, winding four miles through blind curves and stands of pines. You've started early so that the ascent, and maybe part of the descent, will be over before the day's worst heat. You pretend to stumble on scree, send rocks clattering in hopes that any bear wants to avoid you, too.

§

In interactions of humans and bears, the bear always loses. Once prolific, grizzly bears number about 55,000 in North America, of which about 550 range through the Yellowstone/Teton region. Even on protected turf, if a bear's unwanted, too familiar, a "problem bear," then it's removed. But if a bear's tasted human blood – even the blood of a very stupid human, one who deserved to die, was clearly begging to die, erasing all trace of his idiot DNA from selection – the bear dies, hunted down and killed.

§

About as far up the trail as you can climb without actually pressing on to scale Grand Teton's mighty teat, you will reach Surprise Lake, glacially blue with cold, a lovely site to pause, picnic, refresh. About a mile before you reach it, a group of campers scampers past, surprising you, infectious with fear averted – "Bear!" "Grizzly?" you call after them. No, a small black bear who ambled up to help himself to their hung rucksacks as they waded the lakeshore. They turned at the sound of it tearing through canvas to get at the sun-softened string cheese and apples inside. They shout short answers to your questions as they descend. Not sure if it's a baby. Not sure if it's got a mother. You want to turn and scurry back down the mountain, too.

A__ is elated – bear! "We'll be careful." He wants to press on. You think about leaving him there and hiking down alone, but you have the water and he has the keys to the car. After a few moments of arguing, you relent, like he knows you will, like you always do, and you both press on, though more slowly. A's water is gone; you've been slipping him sips of yours, but the afternoon return trip will be hiking downhill, which can be harder, which will be hotter. You creep past pines and shrubs and startle upon, are startled by, the shoreline of the glassy, glacial lake, frigid in midday sun. You scan the currently bearless landscape. Despite the campers' recent experience, you unpack food. You eat quickly while A__ frames photographic scenes with his fingers. Beautiful scenes, but which contain no bears. We should go while there's no bears, you say, packing up.

§

During your descent, the switchbacks seem more sun-exposed. In the heat, the wilderness has grown focused, intent, more silent but for the August grasshoppers buzzing the cheat grass. You hear no birds, but then again, you are distracted by the difficulty of bracing on scree, thighs burning, your toes jammed against the toes of your boots, rubbing raw. Water gone, you try not to feel the fur of your tongue.

§

In interactions of humans and bears, the human will always lose. Only 1-3 humans die each year from a grizzly attack – you're way more likely to be hit by lightning. Because close encounters are rare, are discouraged, you're most likely to die in late summer, if you surprise the bear, and if you run. Then all that speed and claw size and jaw pressure comes into play. The best you can do is try to protect your head and neck.

§

Out of the endless quaking of aspens, the trail opens on a steep alpine meadow criss-crossed by switchbacks. Way in the distance, you see the trailhead – beyond it, the parked cars glitter like clustered beetles. Way in the middle distance, down the hill from you, the brush shudders, divides. Shouldered aside. The grizzly, magnificent. He snuffles in the underbrush, blackberrying. Carelessly, he crushes branches with his great paw, claws at hidden fruit. After a few minutes, he stops feeding, stands up on all fours, then plops down on his butt and scratches an ear with a hind foot, like a big old dog, before resuming his lazy foraging.

A__ already is focused, focusing his zoom lens to bring the bear's image closer. The grizzly lumbers slowly closer, closing the distance. He's easily less than the recommended football-field length away, and you say so to A__, who is shuttering away. "We're uphill, and it's steep. Plus, we're downwind of him," he says and it's true, the tang of bear rides to you on summer updrafts. True, too, that he doesn't seem aware of you, off on his careless business.

You stare at A__, watching him shoot his camera. He has a sweet boyish absorption in his task, tongue poking his upper lip as he works. That sweet boyishness will quickly turn sulky if you insist he stop, but you can't stop the tears and fear rising in you. Scared and angry, you say "You know, you're never going to do anything with those pictures," which is mean, though true. You find yourself hoping that if it comes to it, the bear will attack and eat A__, not you. Meanwhile, however slowly it happens, the grizzly is nearing.

Suddenly, it looms above you – the truth that your marriage is a fragile thing, too easily crushed, as if by a careless paw. The stink of it makes you recoil. You have never been more terrified.

At some point, A__ will remove the zoom, aware the bear is too close to use it, will snug it into his bag, and will turn to you and say "OK, we can go now." You will descend and, despite switchbacks which cut back below the meadow, you will never see the bear again. You will emerge, legs deliquescing with dehydration.

But for now, he is snapping away, snapping pictures you know will never develop. He went into debt for the camera. He barely can afford film, but not prints. At last count, over two hundred rolls of undeveloped film lay decaying in the hall closet, taking on light. What images do print are ghostly, have phantom limbs that still itch and tickle you from time to time. For now, he pretends that he will print these shots, that they will be professional quality, worthy of *National Geographic*. Yet you encourage him, hoping that perhaps by being an advocate for his art, he might become more supportive of yours. In nine years, he will attend exactly one of your readings. In nine years, you will go on many hikes together, and when you leave, you will miss these treks. When you leave, your soul will remain suspended in silver colloid on the hall closet floor, your ghost wandering his underworld still.

For now, the bear is still downhill, upwind.

§

The wind is shifting. The bear is approaching.

MORPH: LUCID DREAMING

I.

Morpheus is the Greek god of dreams who appears in Ovid's *Metamorphoses*. He sleeps in a cave of poppies from which the dreams he creates emerge each night like bats – true dreams flow through a gate of horn and false dreams through a gate of ivory. Nightmares may pass through either.

Morpheus is the captain of the *Nebuchadnezzer* and is obsessed with finding the One destined to end the human-machine war in *The Matrix*. In another life, another reality, I camped hours outside a movie theater with my then-husband A__ to view it. Morpheus seeks out a hacker named Neo and offers him the truth of the Matrix in the form of two pills, two gates. True or false: instead of waking up, Neo enters a new, different dream.

II.

Mark Sandman felt an affinity for Morpheus, God of Dreams, so much so that the Sandman named his band Morphine. Not a user – heroin unchic – he nonetheless needed the analgesic of music, its cure for pain.

His brooding voice, paired with his slide bass and bandmate's baritone sax, thrummed the body at a subconscious, subsonic level, fibrillating the chest. A year after I saw them in Vegas, seven years after I lost my virginity to A__ in his dorm room while Morphine's dreamy blues slurred from the speakers (music which did not shield me from feeling pain), Sandman's chest shattered onstage from a massive heart attack.

III.

Death and Dream. A fan of Neil Gaiman's series *The Sandman*, a comic book that anthropomorphized the metaphysical into gorgeous Gothic entities, A__ planned to dress up for Halloween as the titular character, Morpheus. At 6'7" he could pull off the tall, gaunt figure of the Lord of Dreaming. He asked me to go as Dream's sister, Death.

Our first couple's costume. And, yay! – in the college-girl cliché of slutty costumes, I'd get to go as a slutty Goth! I already owned the ankh necklace, black bodysuit and umbrella, the Doc Martens. I searched vintage shops for a top hat. I practiced lining an udjat eye just right. And I looked perfect.

Too perfect. His roommates – fanboys themselves – gasped, asked me to pose for pictures with them. A__, in plastic cape, moussed hair, and chalky whiteface crumbled, pouted all night. He broke up with me the next day. We got back together, but he continued to break up with me about every six months after that.

I still own a Tarot deck comprised of *Sandman* imagery. I foresaw none of this, despite the fact that before every breakup, before our eventual divorce, I would dream he was leaving me. When I'd awake, crying, my Morpheus would say it was a dream. True or false?

SHE GOT SAUCE

It takes 8 minutes and 20 seconds for the sun's light to reach your tomatoes, the ones you had to wait until June to transplant outdoors. You had to wait until late August for them to soak up all that sun to ripen, and as they did, you lined the windowsills until you had enough tomatoes and enough time to squeeze and freeze them.

At night, after your son has gone to bed, you put New Order on Pandora, put a pot of water on to boil, fill a glass with gin and tonic, and fill the sink with cold water and ice. You weigh the tomatoes, cut an X in the end of each, and drop 8-10 of them at a time into the pot. After a minute, you ladle them out and transport them to the ice bath where, submerged, their skins unfurl like flowers. You drop more into the pot, then back over to the sink where you pluck tomatoes up and peel a few. Shuttling back and forth between pot and sink, you sing "Bizarre Love Triangle" and add more ice to the sink as needed and add more ice to your gin as needed. The peeled tomatoes are slick, so you are careful as you core and halve them, though twice you slip and slit the tip of your finger, which stings in the acid juice. Bent over the trash, you squish out the seeds and juice, toss the halves into a colander to drain. When done, you bag and tag the tomatoes with date and weight. After a few nights of this, your back aches from bending over, your feet from the tile. And your lovely kitchen, the one whose trim you lovingly painted white for a clean look – and it is a clean look, so long as it is clean –

looks like an abattoir. Gin helps. New Order helps. But what helps the most is knowing you have 45 pounds of home-grown sun-ripened tomatoes in the freezer ready to be turned into sauce.

One cool Saturday in early October, you will put all the bags of frozen tomatoes in the sink to thaw, and fill the huge enamel canner with water and put it on to boil. It will take hours. You divide the tomatoes between two stockpots to cook down. It will take hours. You have plenty of time to sterilize jars and lids and get everything organized. You do not have plenty of burners, so this takes a little juggling and some creative use of the dishwasher's hot rinse cycle. The canner is humming a bit but not yet boiling, and the sauce could be thicker. Have some coffee. Go play with your son. Water the houseplants. When the canner lid starts rattling and steam spits out sideways, it's time. Ladle the sauce into the jars, and top off with two tablespoons lemon juice, to prevent spoilage. Wipe the rims and lids and screw shut. Carefully place the jars into the rack, the rack into the canner, replace the lid, and return to boiling. More waiting: 45 minutes until they'll be done. Check email. Check Facebook. Check your checking account. When they're done, remove to a heatproof surface and let cool overnight. It's OK if your heart leaps a little every time a jar pops, letting you know that this age-old yet seemingly magical process has worked, has actually worked the way it's supposed to. Label them and line them up on a shelf in the basement. Stand back and admire them, alongside the carrots and green beans and preserves you put up earlier, tell yourself you could totally provide for your family if you had to, out here on the prairie, even though you secretly know that you would all be dead by November.

One frigidly Arctically brutally cold Sunday in January when you can wait no longer, use one of those jars. Maybe two. Don't waste them on some common spaghetti where you won't really taste the tomatoes. This occasion calls for something special, something worth the effort. Pull out your recipe for pork ragú. Make a list. Go buy a two-pound loin, some onions and rosemary. Don't forget the wine. Open the wine as soon as you get home and pour a glass. Chop the onions. It's OK if you cry. Strip the needled leaves from the rosemary and chop. Stop to smell the scent of it on your fingers. Salt and pepper the loin, and sear every side in a good amount of olive oil. Remove the meat and add

51

the onion and rosemary, using the juice released from the browning onion to help scrape the pot. Time to open the jar; do not rush this moment. Break the seal. Smell deeply, tomatoes as fresh as the day you picked them. Pass the jar to your son, your husband. Smell deeply. Try to remember summer. Before you burn the onions, return to the kitchen and add the tomato sauce. Return the loin to the pot and let the meat braise, filling your house with its savor. When it's falling apart, roughly shred the rest of the meat and stir into the sauce. Serve with big noodles, something that can take it – mafalda or rigatoni – and lots of freshly grated Parmesan. And more wine. It will take you a little over eight minutes to down the first plate. Stop. Lick your lips. Take a sip of wine. Note how the acid of the tomatoes, the wine, balance the rich fat of the pork melted into the sauce. Try to eat the second plate more slowly.

ANATOMY OF AN OUTRAGE

General Anatomy

From my garden-level window, I see legs. Two bodies in the bushes. Guns.

I'm back in my office after my afternoon graduate poetry class at the University of North Dakota where I've kicked off my heels. My feet hurt, and I'm rubbing my eyes as I'm answering emails in the early dark of early March, 2016. The movement just past my gleaming screen draws my tired eyes.

Instantly, I'm awake. Two guys in camo with guns. Active shooters. I can't see where they've gone. I grab my phone and duck under my desk, invisible from the window, dial 911. I tell the dispatcher what I saw, where I am. What she says next hurts my head: she tells me to stay on the line while they check if it's ROTC doing maneuvers – she says it probably is, but no one's cleared it with EMS, so they're sending an officer to check. She thanks me for calling, says I should always call.

My stomach hurts. Too much coffee. Too much adrenaline. Too many times in the last year waiting for friends to check in from campuses locked down during shootings. I realize I'm crying.

She checks back in - yes, it's just ROTC. But it's still good I called. Thanks for calling.

I'm still under my desk holding my phone when it rings again. When I pick up, it's a university officer this time, calling me back—not to reassure me, but to scold me for calling 911. He says ROTC has permission to do this exercise. When I tell him that this was news to 911 and that they encouraged me to call whenever I see a gun on campus, he seems exasperated, and tells me to take it up with ROTC. So I do.

You should know that I left a less-than-professional voicemail with ROTC. I said "fuck" a couple of times. I described what I had seen, then said there was "no fucking reason why I should be terrorized like this. . .to look up and see gunmen on the quad. . .thinking that perhaps we're under attack. There is no reason in this day and age that you need to do these exercises on the middle of the quad. Do them somewhere else. I shouldn't have to work in a terrorized environment. Please don't do this again." You should also know that I left that voicemail less than ten minutes after the incident, still full of adrenaline and fear and righteous rage. So, "fucking" and "terrorized" - remember these. They will come up later.

Digits, Digital
And, later, I wrote a Letter to the Editor at my local paper, in which I say:

> *Apparently, it's not enough that UND's administration is attacking the quality of education by cutting programs and experienced faculty and jacking class sizes. Now, we must also feel under physical attack as well.*

After describing the incident, the response from 911, and the lack of support from the university police officer who called, I conclude the letter with the following:

> *He also tells me that ROTC will be doing these exercises for the next couple weeks.*

> *So I reply that I guess I'll be calling 911 for the next couple weeks—and I will. Every time.*

It's not my job to decide whether people carrying guns at school are an actual threat. It's my job to teach and to get home to my family.

It's already highly inappropriate to conduct unnecessary military maneuvers in the middle of the quad. But with school shootings on the increase and tensions at UND running high, it's especially irresponsible.

We're already under financial and emotional attack. We don't need to feel under physical attack, too.

I wrote this letter on a Friday night in March. The scene I described had happened the previous day, around 4pm. And honestly, I would still have been angry, but wouldn't have written that letter except for two things: that scolding follow-up call from the campus police, who told me to take it up with ROTC, and a sequence of emails exchanged with the ROTC commander Friday.

The ROTC commander emails me in reply to my voicemail, calling it "aggressive and inappropriate." He says the rifles were not loaded, and implies I am unpatriotic, adding, "I thank God every night for those ROTC students that in the near future may be called upon to defend our country and preserve our way of life." He claims that his email is "not meant to be confrontational" but he has cc'ed my Dean and the Chief of Police.

I respond by assuring him that this has nothing to do with patriotism – that the ROTC students and returned veterans are some of my finest students – but that in the campus climate of school shootings, what's inappropriate is to perform these drills in the quad during classes.

When he replies that I have "strong opinions," I say that it's "reprehensible that wanting to feel safe in my workplace is viewed as a strong opinion." Clearly, we are at an impasse.

So, I wrote this Letter to the Editor. And it went unprinted.

Then, ten days later on a Monday morning, it runs.[1] Tuesday evening, a friend who works for the news service that owns both the Grand Forks and Fargo papers texts to say that the local shock jockey whose blog they

55

run has posted about it. I look it up, and sure enough he has, distorting the events and running it with a stock photo that shows ROTC cadets in full dress uniform in parade formation with bayonets, as if to suggest that was what I had seen out my window.[2] I laugh and repost the link on Facebook, where my friends and I joke about it.

The next day, I fly to Virginia to give a reading. Overnight, other right-wing blogs repost the story and it goes viral, appearing on Glenn Beck's The Blaze, Reddit, and an NRA-associated page.[3] At the book festival, my phone vibrates and vibrates. This was hilarious until suddenly it isn't. Local TV wants to interview me, but I'm in transit most of the day. I do release a statement that's read at the end of the coverage, but in my absence, the main voice is the ROTC commander's. As a result, the slant is very patriotic, pro-ROTC, and I'm somehow anti-ROTC.[4] And the news plays the voicemail.

They play the voicemail.

At this point, it is thirteen days after the initial event, thirteen days after I left that voicemail. The ROTC commander has hung on to this voicemail for thirteen days, for just this moment.

When I return, I do a long interview for the newspaper with a reporter I respect,[5] in which I try to do damage control by insisting that I did not call 911 on ROTC - I called 911 on two gunmen in the bushes on the quad, as I had been trained to do in a possible active shooter scenario. I apologize for using profanity in the voicemail in the heat of the moment, but I stand by my assertions that the drill had been unwise and irresponsible.

The convergence of me being out of town and unable to control the story from the start, combined with an otherwise slow news week, even for North Dakota, means this story won't disappear anytime soon. People start posting my contact information online - thankfully, only publicly available work contacts - but there are threats. The police arrange security and surveillance, and we leave town for the weekend. I am receiving hundreds of messages each day.

Immune System: Viral Load
My husband Evan was out of town when the initial incident happened, when the email exchange with the ROTC commander happened, and when I wrote the letter to the editor. I remember distinctly thinking, as I hit "send" on the submission, that I was glad he wasn't home, because he would have convinced me not to do it.

One of Evan's best friends manages the online presence of the local news service InForum. InForum owns both the Grand Forks and Fargo papers, and serves as the server host for the shock blog that posted the first distortion of the incident. They could feign journalism on one hand, and with the other, encourage clickbait. They had a distinct interest in having it go viral. Evan's friend had a distinct interest in watching it go viral, from a professional standpoint, even as he was personally horrified.

Circulation
Out of the 500 or so emails I receive (not counting voicemail and Facebook messages), most are hatemail, most calling for my job.

Nearly all the hatemail (98%) is from men.

Most of the hatemail accuses me of one or more of the following: being anti-military, anti-gun, and liberal:

> *I agree the police should be called...but not on the ROTC trainees, but on you for the size and shape of your nasty nose.*

> *GO FUCK YOURSELF, LIBTARD BITCH! If you don't like the second item in our original Bill of Rights, maybe you should get the fuck out of this country, did that ever occur to you?*

> *Have a nice day,*
> *Haywood Jablomey*

§

> *Mrs. Czerwiec you are an embarrassment to America! If your husband had any backbone at all he would have corrected you on your emotional*

ROTC issues and told you to shut the hell up. Please resign your position as an educator so America will be better off. The amount of emotions you have are astounding. The good people in North Dakota should picket your school demanding your resignation for lack of intelligence. I will be sending UND an email next requesting them to discharge you due to your lack of intelligence. Have a shitty day.

§

Ms. Czerwiec,

I have read that you seem to think that ROTC students with fake guns practicing on campus are a threat to you. Because of this, you seem to think that it is your duty to call the police to waste their valuable time to "investigate" your delusions of fear and rage.

I do hope that you realize that you are a complete fool and worse, a tool of the liberal/socialist/democrat (LSD) wacky left if you in any way think that ROTC students with fake guns practicing on campus are in any way a threat to you.

My son is an active member of the JROTC in his high school and plans on following my footsteps into the U.S. Air Force as I followed my father's footsteps, retiring after 26 years in service in 2011. There is no finer service to a nation than the people who volunteer to protect and preserve the nation against the enemies of the world. You might want to give it a try if you actually had any idea what service meant.

Sincerely, [name redacted], MSgt, Retired, United States Air Force

I respond to every single piece of email I receive, mostly with a template explanation that I tweak as necessary:

Thank you for your message.

Much of the information being dispersed on this incident is misleading. We have a gun-free campus. I saw two young men with guns outside my office. They were not obviously part of any training, and we had not been *notified there would be any training that day. I called 911 to report it in order to protect myself, my students, and my coworkers. 911 was glad that I did, as they had not been notified of training either.*

I have nothing against ROTC or its cadets – they are some of my finest students. But in this current climate of school shootings, I'm sure you would agree that having students run across campus with guns while classes are in session is unwise and irresponsible.

When I said I would call 911 again, I was saying that any time I see something suspicious that is not obviously part of a drill, I will call it in. At the university, we are told, "if you see something, say something." I am doing my job.

Dr. Heidi Czerwiec

I do engage with follow-up emails if it seems appropriate, or the person seems open to it.

Most don't reply.

Some do. For some of those who do reply, it's like my explanation doesn't matter. The (anti-)narrative is more important to believe, as if they need it to feed their outrage, the same outrage and anti-narrative belief that governed the concurrently running 2016 presidential campaign.

However, most of the people who reply seem surprised and even impressed that I've responded, as if startled to discover a real human being behind the veil of online anonymity. Of those, the vast majority are or had been in the military and thought I was anti-military – after hearing my explanation, most agree that calling 911 had been reasonable, and several apologize for any initial belligerence:

Thank you for responding. I overreacted to information found on news websites posting this story because as a military officer I have experienced significant negative encounters with civilians who don't understand what we do.

I was wrong to insult you without knowing all the information and I apologize.

Many acknowledge they had read an account on some blog that had represented the incident in a much worse light. Some sound sheepish for having believed it.

> ......*if this is true then I owe you an apology.....you must know that conservative websites delight in stories that suspect professors of being liberal hozers......likely from stories like the foolishness that went on at mizzou.....it is reported as "just another example" of the progressive incremental sliming of our history, heritage and, perhaps most importantly, our children.......stand up of you to answer.......*

Adrenal Glands

The constant adrenaline gets to me – I can't sleep, and I subsist on coffee. I get dehydrated further by crying and diarrhea. I lose weight.

The way my office design is situated sits me with my back to the door – I take to keeping the door shut, even during office hours, so visitors must knock. Every shadow across it unnerves me. I'm on high alert when I walk to and from my car, or across campus for meetings. We're moving – a fact unrelated to this incident – and our house has a For Sale sign outside, so cars often drive slowly past, and this freaks me out.

And then, after shrinking, my body starts swelling, fluid collecting in strange places – my eyelid, my cheek, my neck – only to subside and swell at another site. Online, I discover that these, too, are attributable to adrenaline, are called adrenal edemas.

Arms

Some who reply and are very pro-gun/open-carry choose to focus on the gun issue – while they agree that it may have been a valid response to call 911, they are more concerned with the campus being gun-free, and spend much of their replies trying to persuade me that guns on campus make everyone safer, and I should have been carrying:

> *Thank you for replying. It sounds like the media has some of their facts wrong.*

> *Short of the complete removal of the 2nd amendment from the constitution, there aren't many options.*

If we can finally get laws where law abiding citizens are allowed to carry guns on campus (as they are now in NC and TX), we may be able to solve some problems. Criminals and those seeking violence will always have guns and carry them wherever they desire. "Gun-free zones" are specifically targeted by criminals because they know they are safe zones for their murderous rampages. No one will be there to shoot back.

That is why the CO movie theater murderer, James Holmes, chose that particular movie theater. That is why the TN military recruitment center shooter chose that location. If law abiding citizens are allowed to carry on campus, there is a defense.

I have been around firearms since I was a child. I shot my first firearm at the age of four. In the southern United States firearms are as common as loaves of bread. More people need to be educated in the proper use and safety measures required by firearms. As I said before, short of removing the 2nd amendment from the constitution, there are not many other options.

(If I should arm myself to defend my campus, does this mean they think I should have shot those boys?)

(And if I had shot those boys, what then? Would they have defended me for defending my school and my self, defending my Second Amendment?)

(And if I had shot those boys)

(. . .)

Brain
When in the midst of a media shitstorm, your training in rhetoric is crucial. You have to control the message. Stick to your speaking points. There is no room for subtlety.

My main point: this was never about ROTC. I called 911 on what I thought was an active shooter on campus.

The media needed it to be a battle. It becomes me versus ROTC.

In order to stick to my main point, I have to insist it is not about ROTC. I have to say that some of my finest students are cadets, which is true. I have to say that some of my finest students are returned veterans, which is true. I have to say that gun-carry issues are moot because we have a gun-free campus – also true.

There is a lot I cannot say.

I do not say: at first I thought this was hilarious. Until it wasn't.

I do not say: the ROTC commander is the one who made this a Versus. He held on to a private voicemail for almost two weeks. During that time, he played it for some students (which I know from dated emails), then released it to the media after the paper printed my letter. But if I say these things, it will play into The Versus.

I do not say: I am against ROTC's presence on campuses, which had been in decline after Vietnam and during "Don't Ask, Don't Tell," but had a resurgence once that policy was repealed and once tuitions rose aggressively. I don't like the militarization of the university. I don't like the aggression. I don't like how it desensitizes us to violence, to seeing guns.

I do not say: I am anti-gun. The gaslighters like to use big words, diagnose me with "hoplophobia," as though this is irrational. But you're supposed to be afraid of guns. That's the point of guns.

I'm averse. Versus. Verses. Writing is how I cope.

Uterus, Genitalia
I know that a woman speaking out online, especially when she challenges power, is a dangerous thing. But still, I'm surprised by how gendered the discussion is.

Many of the emails launch into me without addressing me, but of those that do, most use "Miss" or "Mrs. Czerwiec," a few "Ms.," some "Heidi," and several even "Madame" or "Ma'am" (ironically), "My Dear Woman," or "Missy."

Many of the emails call me cunt, bitch, cow, sow, hope for my rape, say I shouldn't be influencing young minds – my students' or my child's. They challenge my mothering, threaten to call Child Protective Services.

I am gaslit. The word "hysterical" and references to mental illness and overreaction are constant.

Many of the emails equate me, and whatever they've decided I represent, with weakness, effeminacy, with the "pussification of America." While not all of them identify my teaching subject – English – correctly, they attempt to invalidate me by association with other "Liberal" liberal arts: Professor of Art, Professor of Communications, "Professor of Pussies" as one puts it.

I am what is wrong with America. I am what's Left. The young men with their guns are what's right.

I can't help but set this against the 2016 presidential campaign occurring concurrently. Some even reference it in their messages: "I'm sure you're 'All in for Hill' as the idiot liberals say, and yet you know zero about politics and the evils of the Democrat Socialist Party...." This is a campaign in which one candidate brags of grabbing women by the pussy, encourages the "Second Amendment people" to "do something to stop" his opponent – the first party-nominated female candidate in our history – and blasts her as a "nasty woman."

Face
My appearance is mocked, usually in terms of lack of fuckability.

Many search out my work online, in order to mock it. In particular, bad reviews – which Amazon will refuse to take down and which do not specifically describe the quality of my work but which insult me and reference ROTC – are left for my book, *Self-Portrait as Bettie Page.*

The cover image is a photo of me with my Bettie Page back tattoo.

Bettie Page was a Fifties pinup who did work in early bondage and fetish photos.

To write the book, I had to study a lot about fetishes.

Gun fetishes are a little obvious, don't you think?

Spine

I do receive support. Mostly from teachers: faculty at my own university glad that someone spoke up, professors from elsewhere, and teachers in K-12 – all of whom, like me, wonder each day if this will be the one a gunman makes a tragedy of our workplace. Some of them had already lived through that horror. From my grad students, furious on my behalf, who police online threads, Rate My Professor, my Amazon page, mount incensed defenses, for which I am abashed and grateful. Ministers. An emergency preparedness specialist and a SWAT team member, both saying I'd played it by the book. The SWAT team member adds if it had been him, he might have shot those boys. (...)

I do not receive any support from university administration.

It takes a month before anyone contacts me to meet with me – the interim president, after the main outrage is over. And yet during that month they send out statements that amount to weak support, mostly containment. They tell me (privately) that the national ROTC organization has admonished the commander (privately). They admit to a communications failure, but then respond by overnotification, as if to thumb their nose: "Be advised, ROTC cadets will be playing a game of capture the flag on the quad today. They will not be in uniform."

They say I have a right to my opinion. You don't say that when you think that opinion has a legitimate point. It's a polite form of dismissal, the equivalent of my Southern friends saying "well, bless her heart."

They also send out individual emails from official accounts to people who complain about me. I know this, because one is screenshot and posted on Facebook as "proof" that my "bosses" think I'm crazy:

> The University will now send a campus notification before each exercise, and we will also notify the faculty member each time there will be exercises. [Is that a typo – did he mean "members" – or did he really mean I would be singled out for notification?]

We hope that the actions of one faculty member will not tarnish the reputation of the long-standing commitment UND has demonstrated to those who serve in our armed forces. The fact is that the University of North Dakota has a long, proud tradition of Army and Air Force ROTC programs on our campus. Some of the finest men and women at UND are ROTC cadets. In fact, UND President Ed Schafer was an ROTC cadet here. In addition, the University is proud that for many years we have been identified as a Military Friendly School, most recently in November when UND was once again named a Top Military-Friendly University by Military Advanced Education & Transition.

They fall over themselves supporting ROTC and the military, doing everything short of sucking their guns.

They note I will be leaving my position at the end of the semester. They fail to acknowledge there is no connection: I had already notified them of my pending resignation seven months earlier, effective at the end of the school year, when Evan graduates from law school and we move to Minneapolis for new opportunities.

Heart
While he has not read the emails or heard the voicemails, I can't protect Evan from anonymous online comment threads. Yes, they bother me, but it's about me, and I'm handling it. Mostly. Or pretending to. But for Evan, people are coming after his family. I kind of get that – the one comment that pisses me off the most is when someone tries to attribute my actions to Evan's liberalism. That's just one comment. But the comment threads Evan reads and the lack of university support has him seething. He tells me he was tempted to punch a colleague who made a veiled comment about me in an elevator. Having worked closely with the university's PR director, he dreads what might happen if he runs into him on campus. His own rage scares me. I text with another close friend of ours who's also furious on our behalf, to express my worry about Evan. Our friend says, "It's like *The Godfather.* I'm Sonny, I want to blow them all away now. Evan's Michael, he won't forget, and he's going to get his revenge one day." Also male responses, also interesting and complicating.

In April, there is a video circulating on Facebook of men reading aloud horrible Twitter comments to the faces of two women sportscasters, Sarah Spain and Julie DiCaro, to whom the comments are directed.[6] The men reading the comments, even though they're not the ones who wrote them, are appalled and ashamed, and apologize repeatedly to the women. The video makes visible the effect of even just a few such comments – much less the endless stream of them that comes with being an opinionated woman online, especially one who speaks about topics typically "owned" by men.

I cry while I'm watching this video. I spoke up online about guns and military action on campus and got hatemail for only a few months, and it wrecked me for a while.

I fantasize a revenge scenario where the university's PR man and its president have to read my hatemail to my face.

Tongue
I am so fucking terrorized. It comes down to that. Remember when I told you we'd come back to those two words? Most of the "controversy" focuses on them.

News media constantly asks if I am sorry for using profanity. Emailers admonish me for using "unladylike" language. The president of the Student Senate, a young man gunning for a political future in a red state, acknowledges that I had a legitimate reason to call 911, yet passes a motion demanding that I apologize for using "fuck."[7] I had said it in a private voicemail, for which I had already apologized both privately and via media interviews. But he wants me publicly lashed, apologizing in front of the student body. I decline his invitation.[8]

Who knew the most effective weapon against military training is to deploy an f-bomb?

But the other deployment I cop to. I'm a writer; I constantly select among the most effective words. Words are my weapon of choice. And in the heat of anger and adrenaline, I deploy the term "terrorize," knowing full well I'm equating the effect of this drill with the "evil" many of these cadets imagine themselves defending against. I do it because I want to provoke them as much as they provoked me. It worked – too well.

And since we're talking about words, I'll also admit: we all read each other accurately. I knew using "terrorize" and my position as a liberal-arts professor would antagonize them. And though my letter and voicemail never specified any of this, they read me, correctly, as liberal, as anti-gun. I could point out I had said none of that, that I had followed protocol, all of which was true. I could say some of my finest students were cadets and veterans – also true, but a deflection: not the same thing as saying I support ROTC and militarization. So while I might have had language on my side, they were not missing the nuances.

In many ways, this is not about the failure of language – it's about how effective language is, both in its lines and between them, the effect it has, and the side-effects.

Fucking. Terrorized.

Pathology Report
Have I brought these effects, and side-effects, upon myself? Do I have a right to write about the trauma this caused me, however (relatively) brief? Others are suffering greater injustices, and in most ways, the fact that I am a white, middle-class, tenured professor protects me from the worst retaliations.

Sejal Shah, in her terrific column titled "Trauma Privilege,"[9] quotes Roxane Gay from the essay "Peculiar Benefits" in Bad Feminist: "What I remind myself, regularly, is this: the acknowledgment of my privilege is not a denial of the ways I have been and am marginalized, the ways I have suffered. . . . Does privilege automatically negate any merits of what a privilege holder has to say?"

I am right to be angry that I was chastised for calling 911 as I had been trained to do in a possible active shooter scenario, and for my university essentially throwing me under the bus to maintain its "military-friendly" designation. I am right to be concerned about the militarization of campuses and the presence of guns leading to complacency – a week after the initial drill, a student is shot on the north end of campus.[10] And while some forms of privilege inoculated me when I spoke up, I am right to be angry about how I was targeted as a woman. I was marginalized and made to suffer in other ways. As Sejal Shah concludes, "Suffering is not a contest; no one wins."

I may be right, but what have I won? My adrenaline hairtriggers now, spikes at the slightest threat. Spikes whenever I sit down to work on this essay – even at my favorite coffeehouse, snugged into my corner seat – as I write, revise and edit, even collate links, I'm right back inside my fight or flight instinct. Or when small flurries of emails resurface on certain holidays that follow – Memorial Day, July 4th, September 11 – or after Election Day, when the trolls resurface to haunt, to taunt me.

In many ways, six months later, I find that I've come back around to the position of our friend who works for the local news service, the one who was both personally horrified and professionally interested by this incident. I'm fascinated. I'm horrified. For me, the horror and fascination lie always in the language, the threat it embodies.

1. You can see the full letter at http://www.grandforksherald.com/opinion/letters/3990525-letter-military-maneuvers-startle-already-stressed-und-campus

2. https://www.sayanythingblog.com/entry/und-professor-threatens-to-call-911-on-every-campus-rotc-drill/ (But don't give this guy extra clicks.)

3. Just Google my name and ROTC – you'll find all you need. But same as above about the clicks, ok?

4. http://www.inforum.com/news/education/3994037-und-professor-odds-campus-rotc-over-drills-guns

5. http://www.grandforksherald.com/news/education/3994383-video-professors-criticism-rotc-drills-und-campus-draws-internet-ire

6. http://www.espn.com/espnw/culture/the-buzz/article/15386258/men-read-horrible-tweets-directed-female-sportswriters-psa

7. https://und.edu/student-government/sr1516-13.pdf

8. http://www.wdaz.com/news/3999670-und-professor-wont-issue-public-apology

9. http://www.kenyonreview.org/2016/04/trauma-privilege/

10. http://www.inforum.com/news/3997016-victims-name-released-grand-forks-shooting

CONSIDER THE LOBSTER MUSHROOM
Being a brief theory of the craft of creative nonfiction

The lobster mushroom, contrary to its common name, is not a mushroom but the result of a parasitic fungus having infested a host mushroom in a peculiar symbiosis. The fungus, *Hypomyces lactifluorum*, typically attacks milk-caps and brittlegills, absorbing them completely and imparting the bright reddish-orange color and seafood-like flavor of a cooked lobster.

Creative nonfiction, too, is a symbiosis of fact infecting art. Or art infecting fact. You become infected by an idea, a topic – open adoptions, fracking, the history of perfume – that absorbs you, imparting its own qualities, until you're transformed, not the same person as before.

Or, you may play the part of parasite – cloak your work, make it take the appearance of another form: an essay disguised as a list, a letter, an index, a diary. A hermit-crab essay. A lobster mushroom.

Or, you may think you're writing one essay, but another essay takes it over, makes it its own. Think you're writing about hiking? Nope, it's about your ex. A piece about the band Morphine and *The Matrix'* Morpheus and the *Sandman* comics? Nope, your ex. This is not necessarily a bad thing. Lobster mushrooms are much more valuable than the mushrooms they infect – about $25 a pound fresh, or $50 dried, at last check.

§

You should remember that both creative nonfiction and lobster mushrooms, like all fungus, feed off of dead matter, are in turn fed off of. You don't always get there first. Sometimes appalling creatures have nested inside it – sometimes stuff you knew was there, sometimes stuff you forgot was there, sometimes unexpected stuff you uncover. You might be cutting through a mushroom when a centipede or earwig or worm crawls out of the hole it's burrowed into the flesh. "Fuck!" you may yell, dropping the mushroom. Now you have to decide what to do next:

a) Sweep the mushroom into the trash. Burn trash. Burn house. No mushroom, no matter how valuable it might have seemed, is worth this toxic invasion.

b) Pick up the mushroom and examine the damage – how deep does it go? Has the nastiness laid eggs? Are there others? You may feel hesitant to give up on the mushroom, but sometimes you have to negotiate the value of the mushroom against how compromised it's become. If there's too much damage, go back to a); otherwise, continue to

c). Remind yourself of two things:

1.   If you can't deal with the mushroom now, it will come back. It will always come back, popping up whether you want it to or no, because it's part of a larger system, mycelia feeding on what's rotten, what lurks, always, beneath the surface. If you decide in the future you're ready to pluck it and make something of it, it will be there, mushrooming.

2.   You don't have to reveal the source of your mushrooms. Few enthusiasts do, going to great lengths to conceal their sites by lying, covering their tracks. But most are happy to share the fruits of their labors, the fruited mushroom, the

finished product, however fraught. You can share, without sharing everything.

d) Decide you have worked too hard for this mushroom. It is too valuable to let go. THIS IS YOUR FUCKING MUSHROOM. Find a way to deal with the damage:

1.   cut it out completely;

2.   work around it. Convince yourself it will be altered in the shaping/cooking of it anyways. Keep what isn't too bad, what you can still use, what's of value. If you can deal with it, so can everyone else.

3.   Take a deep breath and swallow it whole, bugs and all.

§

But here's the thing. The lobster mushroom, the parasitic fungus, has a super power: it infests mushrooms, matter that is otherwise inedible, possibly toxic, and makes it safe for consumption. Palatable. Even delicious.

§

Is this a craft essay infected by a lyric essay, or a lyric essay infected by a craft essay?

FREUDENSCHANDE[i]: PRIV(AC)Y

Is there a word for the unsettling sensation of sitting down on an unexpectedly warm toilet seat, because someone used it just before you and sat there for a good long while? Maybe something in German?

Unheimlichgesitzenüberraschung[ii]

Usually the cool, even cold, of a seat is itself startling, which is why our society has installed carseat heaters in vehicles, or why the tricked-out Japanese toilets like the Neorest 600 feature pre-warmed seats to accommodate your commode comfort. Accommodating. So, if we prefer warmth, why is this experience so unnerving?

Schrecklichwarmsitzplatzgefühl[iii]

It's unnerving anywhere, but never more so than in a public restroom – a sudden, unwanted reminder that we're all sharing the same facilities, as much as we try to ignore it or pretend otherwise. The tear of a tampon wrapper. The multiple unspoolings of toilet paper, indicating a number two, a code brown. A strategically-timed sniff or cough to cover a fart. Stinks that arise, that you feel implicated in, even if you weren't the instigator, when a newcomer enters to a wall of smell just as you're washing your hands.

Unerwartethindenhitze[iv]

The public privy is an uncomfortable, even unwanted reality check on the illusion of privacy. An odd communion in reverse, based not on breaking bread together, but on shedding it. And the unexpected seat warmth is a weird intimacy physically imposed upon us by strangers. A stranger's private space has intruded upon ours, a stranger's privates previously pressed to the same place as our privates. Deprived. A piracy of privacy.

Heißefremdenhinternsitz[v]

And yet, this physically-imposed intimacy is physics. More specifically, thermodynamics. In conduction, heat energy flows from the warmer to the cooler object, the faster-moving hot molecules colliding with slower, colder molecules until they arrive at the same temperature together, vibrating in unison.

Unbequemischintimität[vi]

It's not that different from nonfiction – sharing intimacy with a stranger. Whether you're the writer or reader, intimacies and empathies and energies are flowing between you, across the text, connecting you in ways neither of you expected. Only connect.

But "intimacy" isn't quite right, either. It's too pretty, with its connotations of a welcome secret, an inside joke, a delicious confession/confection shared between friends, intimates. In much of nonfiction, we are welcomed as confidantes, or at least allowed as sympathetic eavesdroppers.

Belichtungschande[vii]

No, what I'm describing is exposure at our most vulnerable. A sense of shame. Some nonfiction shares its author's shame, a shitshow we're invited to witness – not always well-done, not always as welcome. Shock is not shame, nor necessarily confession. But when done well, we feel blessed by the gift of shame shifted to us, a shared burden therefore

73

lessened. We call it brave and we mean both of us, writer and reader, for facing it. We find its face human.

Both experiences – nonfiction and toilet seat – can be weird, even gross. But ultimately human, even sublimely so.

Which is why I praise you, unseen sitter, unmoved bowel mover who, in the course of your courses, shared your warmth with me, intentionally or no. I praise the warmth itself, offered freely, uncommodified, proof of your movement, moving me at the molecular physical level, and at the metaphysical. And I praise you, reader, with whom I in turn share my warmth, breaking the illusion of privacy, breaking the fourth (stall) wall, to convey this, a love commodious, to you.

---

i Joyful-shame
ii Weird-sitting-surprise
iii Horrible-warm-butt-feeling
iv Unexpected-butt-heat
v Hot-stranger-butt-seat (not in a sexy way)
vi Unwanted-intimacy
vii Shame-of-exposure

SWEET / CRUDE

A BAKKEN BOOM CYCLE

I

From Teddy Roosevelt's cabin in western North Dakota, as far as the eye could see was sea: the Cannonball Sea, last of the North American interior, brimming with paleobiology, swimming with lithe dinosaurs. Later, Lake Agassiz (the -siz sounds like sea), named for the Swiss geologist who read books of stone in the old epic mode, who posited the immense glacial lake, greater than all Great Lakes collected, fed by the end of the last Ice Age. Later still, geologists tell us all that life went underground: carbon-rich shale trapped beneath aquifer-rich sandstone trapped beneath nutrient-rich soil. And buffalo grass: a species whose fine roots lace to dense sod seven feet deep.

What lies beneath you?

(This is all connected.)

Labeled the Great American Desert on old maps of hostile horizons, the Plains become a place that settlers bypass on their way out West seeking the auguries of timbers, pilgrims bristling with hoop-iron and axles. Until a blacksmith named John Deere invents steel plow blades that can break through sod to soil beneath. Until the Homestead Act claims "rain follows the plow." Until settlers staking their claims realize the previous claim is buffalo shit, but learn to tap the aquifers, to siphon off for farming. Until Henry Bakken, a farmer in western North Dakota, taps oil until no more seeps out. Until a U.S. Geological Survey estimates the shale holds 7.4 billion barrels. Until they learn to frack.

Given enough time, a sea can become a desert; given enough time, even a desert has value.

II

Given enough time, an inland sea can become a desert; given enough time, even a desert has value. The Fertile Crescent has been called the cradle of civilization, of incunabular vocabulary, inventing the alphabet so I can tell you these things. Inventing the wheel, literally. Inventing agriculture by irrigation, diverting two rivers to preserve a land alluvially lush. Lavish: a king deviates the Euphrates to water cascading terraces of fruited trees for the pleasure of a favored concubine longing for the meadows of her Persian mountains. Crescent, the sweet kisses she lavishes on his brow.

Today, the gardens are legendary. Today, less than a tenth of the crescent's fertility remains, almost completely dried up, scrub marking the ancient shore, its gardens gone underground, its only liquid sweet crude. Double-edged sword that continues to support and yet thwart civilization, its foreign hungers and wars. Its land increasing in demand, increasingly wasted, unstable – some in ways we've been implicated, participated. I fill my car even as I listen to NPR, my fool deity, my black idolatry. Men's covenants are brittle.

Don't blame us, the oil companies say. It's the Taliban's fault, they claim, as people in the streets raise signs that read *No Blood for Oil.*

III

No blood for oil implies distance, implies foreign. But this is here, this is North Dakota (trademark: Legendary!), one of the worst states for workplace safety. Blame the Wild West culture of risk. Blame an influx of green employees with no industry experience, disordered recruits afoul outcountry. Blame fatigue from long shifts – 12-hour days for 2 weeks straight, mud effigies jagged with blood among the dull clank, the blackened pools of grease – work that goes on regardless of weather. (Don't blame us, the oil companies say, it's the contractors' fault. Don't mention drug use: word is, they skimp on testing to fill out their crews.) Nearly all state fatalities investigated by OSHA occur in the Bakken: two-thirds are pulled into pumpjacks or set afire. (An employee was changing valves when a tank ruptured, soaking the employee in oil; he burst into flame and died as a result of his injuries.) One-third killed in falls or "struck by" hazards. (An employee was hit by a set of power tongs on a rig and died as a result of his injuries.) The death rate in North Dakota is 18 times higher industry-wide. (Word is, it's bad luck to wear another man's hardhat; word is, you have better odds of winning the lottery than getting a visit from a regulatory industry; word is, the payoff is up to $300,000.) None of this includes the near-daily occurrence of truckers sliding off slick highways glassy and treacherous, the force of 40-ton tankers colliding with cars on the back roads of North Dakota: flyover, but not foreign.

IV

North Dakota is a foreign country. Alien. A flyover state, even from space. When we show our foreign friend a photo of a satellite flyover, he's astonished. At nightfall, light clusters on the frozen prairie, phantom city emerged from among the ghost towns. A blooming midnight meridian. Stars in a lake of blackness, a constellation of ignited eyes. The natural gas that emerges alongside the oil costs more to capture than flare. The foreign companies that drill here burn money, a billion a year in flames and fines. A Little Kuwait on the Prairie whose dread watchfires smelter under the dark more brightly than Minneapolis. More broadly than Chicago. In winter, truckers cluster for warmth beneath the flares, which fling their flapping rags of fire six yards into space, toward the stars and satellites and passing planes.

Foreigner, flyover passenger, when you peer out your window, what do you see? What lies beneath you?

V

Q: *What lies beneath you?* A: Plowed prairie. Aquifers left over from the jagged edge of Lake Agassiz' glacial age beneath that. Oil left over from before that, beneath that. "North Dakota is not an industrial State, and the likelihood of serious ground-water pollution resulting from industrial processes appears remote at this time. Groundwater is a renewable resource" (USGS report, 1983). Unless in 2007 that resource is taken out of renewal. Unless that millions of gallons are mixed with a proprietary blend of chemicals exempt from testimony and the Safe Drinking Water Act, a reference to the lethal in it. Unless that mix is injected at high pressure into rock to fracture it, thereby forcing its oil to the surface. Watch it darken and rise. Unless that water, now waste, is rejected, reinjected into disposal wells. Unless that oil and waste water is spilled, leaked, or dumped and contaminates streams and reservoirs. Unless in 2011 the North Dakota Legislature passes a bill that states, simply: fracking is safe. Any word to the contrary is poisoning the well, the water.

VI

The poisoning of their water, their wells, is a primary concern to farmers. More than a thousand spills per year, right in the breadbasket, yet only fifty fines to an industry that polices and pardons itself. What's the solution? Catching them. What's the problem? Catching them. Fracking water ravages farms, seep filling the furrows, slow and perilous. You never see a spill produce again, not even weeds: so toxic it sterilizes the land, poisons animals who drink it, kills aquatic life in wetlands and streams. The crop is wilting as we watch it.

But those plowed prairies converted to overfertilized farmland are prone to overland runoff. The Dutch say fertilizer is good for the father, but bad for the sons. Methane from natural gas fixes nitrogen into anhydrous ammonia, a process fueled by more natural gas. UND (Mining) and NDSU (Agriculture) have partnered to convert flared gas to fertilizer, to satisfy those farmers who require a lot of the stuff – to say nothing of the gas required to power all those tractors, sprayers, and combine harvesters over vast acreages. It takes oil to grease those wheels, to create – between Gas and Ag – a good industrial lubricant.

VII

In the man camps, alcohol and drugs make a good social lubricant, smoothing the (high)way for the thousands of roughnecks, petroleum engineers, pipeline catters, truck drivers, carpenters, contractors, and electricians, as well as journalists, adventure scientists, scholars, and photographers who arrive here daily, driven across the continent onto the prairies. *Two Bakken-bound men on meth head out from Montana.* The men outnumber the women by 30%. Many leave families swimming in underwater mortgages but otherwise safe as houses, while sex offenders and former inmates unemployable elsewhere also come, wayward past disappeared. *Sherry Arnold, math teacher, heads out for her morning run.*

Oil companies erect dormitory-style barracks, with no tolerance for guns, alcohol, drugs, or women – even spouses. Or RVs and trailers populate amenitied lots with attendant attempts to set boundaries, winterize and hunker down for the long term. Then, there are parked pickups and vans and makeshift shantytowns, frail structures insulated with styrofoam, plywood, and hay or what have you against the cold wind's stinging grit, no water or sewage – the smell carries twelve miles outside of town. *Outside of town, her shoe is found.*

Not enough lubrication, and things break down; but too much is a slippery slope: "We got one guy, got in this other guy's camper and he wouldn't leave, so the guy beat the shit out of him." Concealed-carry permits skyrocket: "We never send just one girl out alone to clean properties, and still they get propositioned." With no set boundaries, reported rapes are up 20%. *A farmer finds her body abandoned in his field.* Glen Crabtree, floor hand at a rig, sports a tattoo reading *Fuck, Fight, or Trip Pipe* and he'll do it, too – he'll ride this boom till it busts.

VIII

Boom and bust, through rock, literally. Two miles vertically, then laterally two miles. (What lies beneath you?) Filter socks are prophylactics that catch the flowback from ejaculated fracking water. Which is not water but water, plus a secret blend of chemicals, salts, metals, and "naturally-occurring radioactive material." The new "norm": a hot mess of hot waste, 75 tons per day. The socks discarded in landfills till Geiger counters started clicking insistently, incessantly. After this became unacceptable, after they stopped accepting them, the only place to take them (for a fee) is a facility in far Colorado.

Soon, the socks surface on the reservation, in dumpsters and abandoned buildings, on flatbeds with missing plates. Indian children at play don them, becoming ghosts. Radium conceals itself, too. In young bodies it replaces calcium to honeycomb the bone. It plays a garbled game of telephone with the DNA, lodging in the reproductive organs, the bust. Then, boom.

IX

Then, what seems like boom after boom – the clogged arteries of the Heartland erupt. Over a million barrels cocked and loaded per day discharged by rail to the East, West, and Gulf Coasts, Bakken crude imbued with volatile butane in tankers railworkers dub "bomb cars," that even the DOT terms "an imminent hazard." And 2013 went off the rails: 47 dead in Quebec where sewer covers flung on plumes of flame. Half a million gallons "missing" in three Southern rivers. Fireballs hissing on cinderland prairies above December snows.

Choo-choo, my son says, listening to the whistle blocks from our house. Grand Forks is a switching yard for the 15-plus trains (of which 4 carry oil) that pass through each day, slowing and stopping long enough to be graffitied. In the past, only two have ever derailed. Mostly, they hold up traffic, unspooling slowly, rolling galleries of Midwestern art my son points to, saying *choo-choo*.

Meanwhile, grain piles up – 2013's harvest still in the bins, 2014's in the field – waiting to hop a car to market. Train backlogs of up to two months mean low supplies of Cheerios for us, though the Rails deny being greased by Oil. (To say nothing of Amtrak passengers trapped on delayed trains out on the prairie. To say nothing of the 12,000 truckloads per day struggling singlefile the two-lane Highway 85 from Williston to Watford City.)

This is the economics of gridlock, the toll of increased traffic.

X

The toll of increased traffic: increased trafficking. When Indians were gifted the bad lands no one could grow or graze on, no one knew that beneath the Badlands lay oil. Now, money is coming in, drawn by the crude oil and the jobs to remove it. Now, crime is coming in, drawn by the money and the crude patchwork of jurisdictions that operate there. Numbers that don't work for Indians on the Fort Berthold reservation: the 2 tribal officers on duty who haven't left to run rigs; the 1 substance-abuse treatment center with 9 beds; 911. Operations Winter's End and Pipe Cleaner can't stop the pipeline of heroin and meth from Mexico. In 2012 in New Town, a town known for maybe knife fights at worst, a meth-addled intruder butts into a home with a hunting rifle and into a grandmother and three kids with a hunting rifle, slender instrument bearing brute ceremony, before slitting his throat before deputies. A fourth child survives, hiding under his brother's body.

This happens too, more than we want to think: a Native girl is seduced by her older "boyfriend," her body bought and sold. She is confined to a kennel under a urine blanket and starved, kept high and compliant on heroin, brittle and shattered to a lull. She's called exotic – Indian Princess, Polynesian, Asian, worth a premium – on Backpage.com's bill of particulars, easier than ordering a pizza. If she tries to get help, she might be beaten or killed by a pimp who is careless with women's bodies. If she tries to get help, she might be arrested in a state that couldn't care less about women's bodies, yet regulates them more often than oil.

This is how the vulnerable survive: by lying under another body (*what lies beneath you?*); this is happening to too many children.

XI

So many children being born! North Dakota remains the only state whose population was larger in 1930. After eight decades of outmigration, now sudden labor and growing pains, towns whose numbers have quintupled. Two-thirds of that has been transient – workers wending homeward after two-week shifts – but as housing is built, families come with. With 3,000 more students, they need more buildings, buses, and teachers who, like schoolmarms of old, must shack up in classrooms or with students' families. McKenzie County needs $200 million to repair its weathered and broken corridors overrun with overweighted, overfreighted trucks driving overtime. The resulting accidents and crime cause a spike in 911 calls, but it can take eight hours for EMS to reach you across that fever of prairie. If they have to navigate the maze of mancamps, your crisis may be unlocateable. Increased demands on water (both public and industry), sewer, inspectors of all sorts, and social services— Even WalMart which, with lack of local entertainment has become the de facto town hall of its milling citizenry, needs 200-some employees at $18 an hour, can't keep shelves stocked, won't bother to unpack pallets, just wheel them out and watch six-dollar milk disappear.

Oil revenues remit directly to the State (I picture a building with a big money-stuffed mattress in the basement), who returns only about ten percent to those counties. To be fair, they're betting on the inevitable bust, to not be left holding the bag once drilling becomes production and most of these men leave, leaving a mere few prairie anchorites manning pumps. We don't need more ghost towns. The State is averse to invest in infrastructure, so even after an emergency $1.2 billion, the roads are still clogged, potholed and buckled, a rough ride for all the new Rough Riders, the school classrooms still too full.

XII

The classrooms are empty. The campus, decamped. Over a third of Williston State's faculty have fled for lack of affordable housing, for their families' safety. Besides, there are few students left to teach. The young men figure they'll work the rigs for a few years, save enough to pay their way through school debt-free. And who can blame them? The women are afraid to be women in this wild west. The public campus is encamped by the public. Shrouded figures shuffle like a cortege past dorms, desperate to enter. Most, grit perched in their ears, jaws a seizure of cold, just need a hot shower, need to feel human again. But the women, trapped just inside the passcoded doors, don't know that, don't believe that. Most go home, though a few flirt with working the sour bars of single men, the strip clubs where it's said you can make $2,000 in tips per night. And who can blame them? Why waste your youth inside a classroom, your time in a shit job, when there's so much money to be made?

XIII

There is so much money to be made. So who's making it? Oil: companies in the U.S., Canada, and Norway – the same Norway from whom many North Dakotans descend, the same Norway extolled as a standard of prudent statehood, who prizes its citizens and is able to do so by indifference to its emigrants' welfare on the prairie. Our government, and therefore you and me: my state's made $34.4 billion, which benefits me way over here on its eastern edge, mostly Minnesotan. Oil's infrastructure: builders, welders, developers. Pipelines: Enbridge, Halliburton, and Hess. Warren Buffett, the Bakken's new railroad baron. The two thousand new millionaires minted per year in North Dakota, owners of mineral rights separate from their surface (what lies beneath you?). With wages up eighty percent for all, McDonald's and Taco Bell can't compete paying even two-to-three times minimum wage, and board up doors. Not banks, who make money off loans but not, ironically, off rich deposits. Land owners. Landlords. Riggers and truckers, called "oilfield trash with oilfield cash." You won't believe me when I say there are guys making six figures who are homeless.

XIV

Sooner or later, everyone here is homeless. The absurd six-figure salaried with nowhere to sleep, sure, but safe as houses is no safe bet. In 2011, the Missouri and Mouse flood thousands of houses. A freak tornado in 2014. Jacked property taxes to fix overtaxed infrastructure. Jacked rents that go for more than Manhattan or San Francisco. Hijacked landowners who discover you don't always own what lies beneath you and don't like the influx of trucks and dust and drills and maybe sterile land. Locals who liked their corner of rural life and just want all these kids off their lawn.

Soon enough, after the boom, in two or twenty or fifty years, the landscape will resume its aesthetics of abandonment. Halliburton will pull up its camps down to the PVC pipe to replant at the next site. Newly-built highway bypasses will bypass Potemkin towns on the prairie. Schools will attenuate, consolidate, then close. Lined waste wells will not leak; concrete will crack, but not picturesquely like weathered wood churches.

But for now, there are pumpjacks and tanker trucks, far as the eye can see.

LAST EXIT

Given enough time, an inland sea can become a desert, a desert can become valuable. For foreign deserts, we say *No Blood for Oil*, and while North Dakota is like a foreign country, a flyover, it's here, now, beneath our feet. *What lies beneath you?* Waters, wells, poison. Lubricants (industrial, financial, social, sexual) help, boom or bust. Busted, the boom takes its toll: increased traffic, increased trafficking. Too many hospitals, jails, and classrooms are full and yet the colleges are empty. There's so much money to be made, and yet no amount of money makes this home. The wealthy homeless wheel through the flare-lit landscape, within sight of Teddy Roosevelt's cabin.

A CHILD OF GOD, MUCH LIKE YOURSELF
A MUTAGENIC FANTASIA

"I will pioneer a new way, explore unknown powers, and unfold
to the world the deepest mysteries of creation."
—Mary Shelley, *Frankenstein*

I. Wormwood, Gall [Chernobyl, 1986, 2011]

He snatched a fire and cocked it. Bang, he said. First, the face vibrates with stinging pins that pierce the skull with white light. *Stippling against snow, he sparked.* A metallic taste of iron sucked, sickening the tongue. Gag, coughing and vomiting as insides deliquesce, atomic bonds unlocking arms, the way a cold front melts or a Cold War melts down, Soviet states of matter breaking up. *He flailed, faultline, and burned absolute in his innards like saints.*

Children play in Ukrainian rain that turns black and oily. A gentle murder. Each child a lit lantern to be blown out: a toddler whose torso blooms into a tumor, *other self fused in a collision;* abandoned boy, *spraddlelegged and ragged,* slithering on a floormat and lapping oatmeal like a whining pack animal, *laborious gargoyle, unlearned;* a girl radiant in the frail sheathing of her throat—unpinned ribbon of tongues, odd steel of grace tonged to the fire's temper—until the doctors cut out her thyroid, glowing Chernobyl necklace. *Winter, outraged, cauterized them young.*

The elderly return, following the trails of mushrooms shining in the forest, find their way back by the lights of their own throats. In the Russia under Russia it is daylight all the time. They prefer to die on familiar contaminated soil than in the anonymity of cities. Around them the forest thrives, crackling alive—the world's background noise increased threefold, *its jaw a galvanized fist chattering*—static hum, hidden in the milk like spilt glitter. They say the lost come back as boars, as luminous deer, as swallows, songs in their scarred throats, *frayed breath a vicious hissing.*

In the zone's irradiated radius, the concrete sarcophagus admits visitors minutes at a time.

II. No Romper Room for Miss Sherri [Germany, 1962]

Little seal, little seed *rutted ill,* you slid through a thalidomide-ridden womb, *homemade jigsaw pieced of slumpshouldered bump,* concealed for days from your mother until your flippers affixed to prosthetics for a gaudy appearance of passing. Beautiful mutant, nubbin shucked bare, night-damp and humped in a dream-midden, middle-aged now and what if no one to remind us of this ghostly treason? What then? *Body shucked bare,* selkie-like, the seal the true skin.

III. Theodore Roosevelt Approves this Message [Eugenics, ongoing]

Everywhere mothers spilt their milk, spilt fetuses they feared, fearing
that ancient threat: that a woman visited with a corrupt birth be with
her brood buried alive, each child a lit lantern to be blown out. *Vicious
hammer, springloaded, sprocketing like an uncoiled snare. Slow occlusion rolling
her to doom.* A severe doom, you will say, and not to be used among
Christians, yet more to be looked into than it is. Sterilize to keep the
life stream pure of some *self-veering mutant, meniscus tilting aswamp.* Cleft
Palate. Anencephaly. Feminism. Negro Criminal Youth. Idiot Brain.
Asymmetrical Face. *Wrong blood, borne up.*

I'm supposed to be here, he said.

IV. Orange Agents, Ready for Round-Up [Red River Valley, 2013]

Closer to home, women miscarry or give birth to genetically-modified organisms near a river whose banks overfloweth with farm runoff, *opaque vitriolic* to prevent more bad biology from breeding in. One baby bleeds out in utero, *blowed tree a shapeless bloom;* another's catastrophic defects cause a cascade of shutdowns, *no way to live in the ordered mistake of his losses. Palmupward, they bore it, crude agrarian figures in a violent mural.* You who have seen death—*a coffin-sized door, canted–*

V. [Fukushima, 2013]

—go now, goddamned.

NOTES

Decants: Much of the background information and descriptions for these perfumes and perfumers comes from several excellent blogs, including *Perfume Posse, Bois de Jasmin, Now Smell This, Perfume Smellin' Things,* and *Basenotes.* In "Use It and/or Lose It," the acronym IFRA refers to the International Fragrance Association.

"Bear": statistics on the grizzly bear's physical characteristics, range, and history of interactions with humans come from the National Park Service.

"Consider the Lobster Mushroom": the websites of the Minnesota Mycological Society and of Alan Bergo's *Forager/Chef.*

Sweet/Crude: A Bakken Boom Cycle: Sources of information for this lyric essay sequence include the following:
Bakken.com, the online industry newsletter

Eaton, Joe. "Bakken Oil Boom Brings Growing Pains to Small Montana Town" *National Geographic.* July 2014.

"The Great Plains Oil Rush." Special series on National Public Radio. Jan.-Feb. 2014.

Horwitz, Sari. "The Dark Side of the Boom." *Washington Post.* Sept. 28, 2014

The North Dakota Man Camp Project by UND professors Bill Caraher and Bret Weber

Sontag, Deborah and Robert Gebeloff. The Downside of the Boom. *The New York Times.* Nov. 11, 2014. -part series.

Numerous articles published in *The Wall Street Journal, Billings Gazette, Star Tribune, Fargo Forum, The Dickinson Press,* and *Williston Herald*

This piece includes language from Cormac McCarthy's novel *Blood Meridian.*

"A Child of God, Much Like Yourself": Sources include Paul Fusco's photo essay, *Chernobyl Legacy* (2010)

Nuclear Nightmares: Twenty Years Since Chernobyl (photos Robert Knoth; reporting Antoinette DeJong)

NoBody's Perfect (2008) a documentary on thalidomide defects, directed by Niko von Glasow

Eugene S. Talbot's *Degeneracy: Its Causes, Signs, and Results* (1898) online at the Medical Heritage Library (MHL)

Bethenia Owens-Adair's *Human Sterilization: It's [sic] Social and Legislative Aspects* (1922) online at MHL

Miss Sherri, host of the children's television program *Romper Room*, had taken thalidomide during her pregnancy and went to Sweden to terminate it. As a result of the news coverage, she was fired.

Italicized phrases are language from Cormac McCarthy's novels *Child of God* and *Outer Dark*. The poem also contains riffs on lines by Lucie Brock-Broido.

ACKNOWLEDGMENTS

Big gratitude to Dinty Moore and Kathryn Nuernberger for their careful and generous attention to this collection.

Wafts of love to Jehanne Dubrow for sending me down the rabbit hole of scent and for reading early versions of some of these Decants, to Moira Egan for her fragrant advice, and to my Women's Poetry Collective – Christine Stewart, Barbara Duffey, Jeanne Emmons, Marcella Redmund, Darla Biel, Lindy Obach, and Norma Wilson – for their feedback on this sequence.

High-fives to Bill Caraher for his unrelenting support of Sweet/Crude, and for the strong prods to write "She Got Sauce" and "Anatomy of an Outrage."

Love and thanks to my Bugout Baggers writing group – Jennifer Bowen Hicks, Katrina Vandenberg, Michael Kleber-Diggs, and Greg Luce – and to Jen Fitzgerald, Chelsea Rathburn, and Anna March for cheerleading and feedback.

And deep bows to Nicole Walker and Lee Ann Roripaugh for their friendship and for showing me a path from poetry to essay.

Much thanks to the following journals and anthologies, in which some of these essays first appeared:

Amethyst Arsenic: "Prohibition Expedition: Stepping Out"
Assay: A Journal of Nonfiction Studies: "Freudenschande: Priv(ac)y,"
The Bakken Goes Boom: an excerpt from 'Sweet/Crude: A Bakken Boom Cycle'"
Borderlands and Crossroads: Writing the Motherland: "A Child of God Much Like Yourself: A Mutagenic Fantasia"
Brevity: "Consider the Lobster Mushroom"
Cherry Tree: "Cuir"
Eleven Eleven: I–IV from "Sweet/Crude: A Bakken Boom Cycle"
KYSO Flash: "5 by (N°) 5"
New Poetry from the Midwest: IV from "Sweet/Crude: A Bakken Boom Cycle"
North Dakota Quarterly: "She Got Sauce"

Oakwood: "Cognoscenti: Germaine Cellier," "*Djedi*," and "The Love for Three Oranges"

Parks and Points: "Bear"

Red Sky: VII from "Sweet/Crude: A Bakken Boom Cycle"

ROAR: Literature and Revolution by Feminist People: "Anatomy of an Outrage"

scissors & spackle: "Fluid" and "Green thought in a green shade"

South Dakota Review: "Morph: Lucid Dreaming"

State of the Art: KYSO Flash Anthology: "5 by (N°) 5" (reprint)

Waxwing: "A Child of God Much Like Yourself: A Mutagenic Fantasia"

"Sweet/Crude: A Bakken Boom Cycle" was published as a chapbook by Gazing Grain Press in 2016.

ABOUT THE AUTHOR

Heidi Czerwiec is a poet and essayist, author of several chapbooks, the recently-released poetry collection *Conjoining*, and the editor of *North Dakota Is Everywhere: An Anthology of Contemporary North Dakota Poets*. She holds an MFA from UNC-Greensboro and a PhD from the University of Utah, and was a professor for twelve years before absconding to Minneapolis, where she is Senior Poetry Editor with *Poetry City, USA*, Contributing Editor with *Assay: A Journal of Nonfiction Studies*, and works with the Minnesota Prison Writing Workshop. Visit her at heidiczerwiec.com

THE ROBERT C. JONES PRIZE FOR SHORT PROSE

Robert C. Jones was a professor of English at University of Central Missouri and an editor at Mid-American Press who supported and encouraged countless young writers throughout a lifetime of editing and teaching. His legacy continues to inspire all of us who live, write, and support the arts in mid-America.

The editors at Pleiades Press select 10-15 finalists from among those manuscripts submitted each year. A judge of national renown selects one winner for publication.

ALSO AVAILABLE FROM PLEIADES PRESS

dark // thing by Ashley M. Jones

How to Tell If You Are Human: Diagram Poems by Jessy Randall

Country House by Sarah Barber

The Darkness Call: Essays by Gary Fincke

Among Other Things: Essays by Robert Long Foreman

Bridled by Amy Meng

A Lesser Love by E. J. Koh

In Between: Poetry Comics by Mita Mahato

Novena by Jacques J. Rancourt

Book of No Ledge: Visual Poems by Nance Van Winckel

Landscape with Headless Mama by Jennifer Givhan

Random Exorcisms by Adrian C. Louis

Poetry Comics from the Book of Hours by Bianca Stone

The Belle Mar by Katie Bickham

Sylph by Abigail Cloud

The Glacier's Wake by Katy Didden

Paradise, Indiana by Bruce Snider

What's this, Bombardier? by Ryan Flaherty

Self-Portrait with Expletives by Kevin Clark

Pacific Shooter by Susan Parr

It was a terrible cloud at twilight by Alessandra Lynch

PLEIADES
P R E S S